brown hijabi belonging

Amina Amjad

BookLeaf Publishing

India | USA | UK

Presentation by *BookLeaf Publishing*

Web: www.bookleafpub.com

E-mail: info@bookleafpub.com

ISBN : 9789357448642

First edition 2022

PREFACE

As a young South Asian woman, with an obvious visible religious background, it is safe to say that it can be an emotional rollercoaster growing and navigating through society – to feel like we belong, to feel like we're enough and that we matter… it has not always been there for us. Battling conflicting expectations, whilst trying to figure out who we truly are, is not a smooth-sailing experience. Processing my journey with poetry has been both beautiful and cathartic. I hope you find peace with anything within this book, whether it's just knowing you're not alone in how you are feeling, through it all, the anger, the sadness, the acceptance, or even just finally realising that you are so damn enough. I want to end this very brief preface by explaining the importance of being content within yourself. This may mean being more South Asian than 'Western' or more Western than South Asian – wherever you are on that scale, there is no right or wrong. It is whatever feels authentic to you. You do not need to answer to anyone except you. You do not need to explain or validate the way you choose to live your life. And you certainly do not need anyone's approval before your own approval.

Body Image

It was really hard growing up knowing that the worldly standard for beauty did not include brown skin... even today we are bombarded with images of women with very specific features... the cute button nose, the big eyes and lips, the hourglass body, clear skin - and of course that is not to say that they are not beautiful, they are. Though let us not forget we ALL are beautiful.

We all have had those brief moments in our lifetime where we have looked deeply into the mirror, dressed our best and have felt so damn gorgeous. I try to carry those moments with me, and not to compare myself to others.

Now I can hear you say "easier said than done!" This I understand. We all slip up from time to time, but it is about bringing ourselves back and working on building our confidence from within. This has taken me 25 years to do. When I was much younger, I would apply the lightest of powder to make my skin look more pale or I would even pinch the tip of my nose to see what it would look like if it were smaller. We have all been there where we have unknowingly allowed our insecurities to consume us. My heart aches for the younger version of myself, but also for the countless others who have felt similar, and perhaps may even do so until this day.

I hope some of the poems here give you some solace. In each chapter you'll notice the poems being set up as a journey… starting off in a not so good place, but ending in triumph. I hope that they remind you you are not alone in how you feel. But also how you can go finding that untapped strength and power inside to help you overcome any negative beliefs you have about yourself. If you are seeking solace, you can find this here. If you are seeking to find your unshakeable self-confidence and acceptance, you can find this too here.

--since when is being brown not
beautiful--

I hear him say "You should see his daughters,
they're all so fair, and so beautiful"
so fair…
and so beautiful…
those words combined, never fail to feel like a
sharp pin
being pricked into my skin
they never fail
to make me wince
this endless tale

In angst
I look in the mirror
knowing I can't change a thing
endear her

I'd like to find the human
who set this standard
who robbed beautiful brown women
of their allure
and their radiance.

I am imperfectly perfect.

Career

It is never easy trying to fight your way into Western society. Especially whilst breaking away from the traditional cultural norms that predominantly approve of women putting domestic duties as their utmost priority. It did not mean they could not pursue education or work, but domestic duties had to undoubtedly remain number one, and if it was not so, then you have failed as a woman.

Often you could find yourself leaving the room thinking there is something slightly wrong with you because you wanted to pursue that passion... that career... that dream. But it was not something you could completely remove from within your soul either. It would always creep back. As if it were a part of you, telling you to respect it.

I would like to point here that not all South Asian/Muslim women have experienced this. One thing we all must stop doing is generalising and we need to combat our unconscious bias. Stop putting us all into one damn box that is labelled 'oppressed'. I am officially ripping that label off.

And another thing which is just as important to remember is that not all women want to pursue careers. And you know what, that is 100% fine, acceptable and fab. We need to stop looking down on women who choose the route that is not something you would agree with. How are we ever to create safe spaces when we carry this self-entitled notion with us and then continue inflicting it upon others.

But let's not let western society off the hook either, no no...because they surely have not created enough spaces for ethnic minorities to rise or have even included them in higher-level conversations. They'll include us for smaller roles as a mere tick box, but it is rare they genuinely action what we have to say, about our experiences and we'll often drift afar into the background... the shadows. It continues to be a difficult process when you are made to be the inferior. So now it's time to continue without them. Now it's time we create safe spaces inclusive for all where we thrive and experience acceptance.

You are not alone in your pain in managing the above conflict. And I hope you begin to start believing in yourself the way you know you should. And if you don't know this, well I hope you know this now. Believe in yourself. Don't give up. Don't cease to other's expectations of you.

I'm not bonus points
for you to achieve diversity
I need you to make
genuine space for me

hear my voice
see my talent
or get out of my way
I'm done being patient

I will never forget that pang of pain,
hearing your mocking laugh,
the sinking of my heart,
when you try to keep me tame

I told you my career aspirations,
to which you said,
"maybe you should focus on marriage instead"

--don't let anyone hold you back--

Chin up
walk with grace
with conviction
don't let them tell you 'your place'

please don't wait for approval
shake what they think to be true
it's the old time cliché
'there's only one you'

Identity

Holding a hyphenated identity is both a burden and an incredible privilege. It mostly feels like the former when you are in the process of figuring out all the intricate details of this hyphenated identity, and then becomes a beautiful privilege once it has all become clear.

In the messiness of it all it can feel extremely isolating and mind-boggling. One minute you think you have it all figured out and then something changes. This is ok, however, as we are forever moulding/changing/growing into new versions of ourselves. Which is something I now realise and have accepted. But growing up trying to find your place in the world, a sense of belonging, was heart-wrenching as you eventually realise that does not exist for you. You had to create it for yourself.

Not to mention the occasional 'keep at arm's length' treatment you would receive from Western society. You were always reminded of your difference to them. The only way to feel acceptance was to essentially drop the cultural aspects to you, and to adapt their way of living. But I did not want to do this, nor is it crucial once you realise you do not need to wait for their approval.

I would like to note again that not all of western society will reject those with a hyphenated identity. There are some kind and pure souls who have done the inner work at battling their unconscious bias and the deep embedded colonial mind-set within. Again a reminder, do not put everyone in the same box.

But going back to the issue at hand - if you feel you need to validate your being to others, you are surrounding yourself with the wrong people. It is time to take back your own internal power and the right to define yourself.

Despite assumptions, critique, and negative stereotypes, I hope you continue being who you are with your hyphenated identity, rather than believing that there is 'one' you must choose. This is by no means easy, but a pursuit that you may be content with.

--i do not belong anywhere--

I was recently told
by someone close to me
that I will never belong,
or feel truly at home anywhere

how I wish they were wrong…

But Pakistan may always see me as an outsider,
this I know already to be true,
but the UK will also never accept me as their
own.
They will never see you.

At first I thought, this is untrue,
The UK is my home,

but growing up as a hijabi
I now realise how I had been 'othered'

it pains me to say
But the truth has now been uncovered

"Are people treating you differently?" is all I
needed to hear from my non-Muslim friend.
It isn't all in your head.

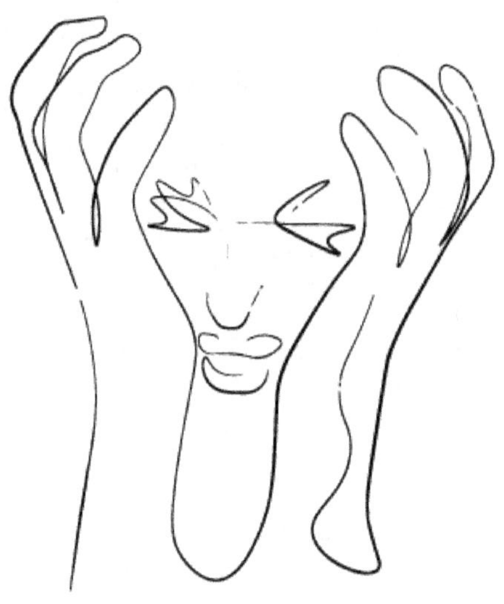

--humanity extends to us too--

Sometimes I feel as if I've finally arrived home
you see my soul has been on a roam,
for a while
but then I'm reminded of how low we're
regarded
we've still not yet been pardoned
for mistakes not our own

we're second citizens
our lives devalued
maybe one day
you'll see us as humans

--you do not get to define me--

Think of me what you will…inferior
Say to me what you will…hurtful
Try to tell me how not to be…oppressed

Just remember
You are not superior
Nor my saviour.
Your approval is not a prerequisite
For my existence.
If your care is genuine
You'll work towards coexistence.

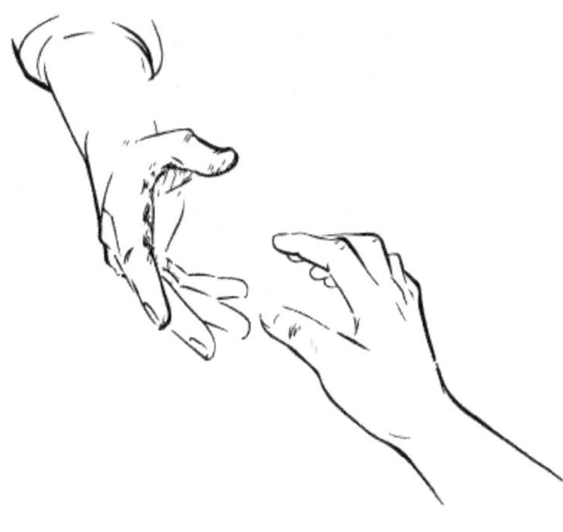

Self-acceptance versus acceptance from others

Self-acceptance is something most humans may struggle with. But let us not begin to explain the struggles South Asian women who wear the hijab may feel when dealing with conflicting expectations from their culture whilst living with Western society. It is a never ending battle, always needing to be shielded and armed in case someone decides to spear you with their unkind words. Their rejection.

The shame you may feel when those within your cultural community look down upon you, for not being e.g. "brown enough" wishing you were different.
Then there is the neglect from society who have deemed you 'not British enough' – again a continuous clash between the two, and at the same time trying to find your own self-acceptance versus the desire of wanting to belong somewhere.

In the chaos of trying to please both sides, you may have lost yourself in the process. You may find you have multiple personas so you can fit in with whatever crowd you find yourself within.

How exhausting that sounds. Constantly over-analysing each and every interaction to make sure you have their approval. The dissatisfaction that comes with this is disheartening, not to mention how unfulfilled you may feel with your inner-self. It is safe to say that it is an extremely under-researched area, and it is not spoken enough on the mental and emotional impact this has on our wellbeing. Leading to feelings of constant frustration, exhaustion and feeling suppressed.

I would like to ask you now to just simply be yourself. You will never fully know how people feel about you – comes to terms with being different to the societal norm and your culture's values. Accept that you may be different, and that is more than acceptable.

--shame--

i wish I could save you,
but I am too busy trying to save myself,
from drowning in self-scrutiny

--how do i become brave again?--

This anger is overwhelming me.
I can feel the flames licking my chest
the fumes in my lungs
the voice within that wants to explode,
to fight,
but I can't.
Because the second I do
I'll be placed in the crossfire,
all guns pointing at me,
to surrender.
It's only then that I realise
how much society has stomped on me,
beaten my spirit,
crushed my pride.
And with that
fear has ripped away my tongue.

--life is too difficult to be pretending--

If only people knew, just how much more
satisfying it is to be busy being yourself, rather
than pleasing others.

--to be me--

I never thought that my biggest battle
was finding out who I am
nor did I knew that my hardest fight
was to be who I am.

Arrival

Here we are, at the final destination. These poems, these feelings, experiences and thoughts have all spanned over a decade at the least. This poem was inspired by Trevor Millum's 'Sad I Ams' - this is actually something I had written when I was 22 years old on my MSc Counselling & Psychotherapy programme. Final reconciling and coming to terms with who I am.

Even if others did not respect, accept, appreciate, value who I was, my choices, my lifestyle, I was finally in a place where I did. And that is all that mattered. I hope this final piece below gives you the push you need to do the same for you, and to stop waiting for other's love.

My adaption of 'Sad I Ams' by Trevor Millum

I am
a hijabi British-Pakistani.
The missing shadow
hidden deep in every nook and cranny.
The lost soul
looking for my home, wandering through dark
alleys.

I am
the treacherous outsider,
who needs to be redeemed,
the spiritless anti-feminist
who's borderline extreme.
But the girl whose family
expects her to be like seraphim.
This hopeless typhoon
drowning, spiralling
from all her broken dreams.

But… I also am,
the lighter of fire in the sky,
the sun-kissed passionate days
all across July,
the bright-eyed child who just hates goodbyes,
I am someone you can't come by.

I am,
the ocean waves hugging the beach sand.
A classical book,
that you sometimes find hard to understand,
But if you pick me up,
I'll kiss your wounded hand,
I promise you,
just get to know me, you'll be glad.

But if you don't what to know who I am,
that's okay,
I'll patiently wait for that day.
And I'll be busy loving myself along the way.